Abraham Lincoln: 65 Fascinating Facts For Kids

Max Rogers

This book is just one of a series of "Fascinating Facts For Kids" books. For more fascinating facts about people, history, animals and much more please visit:

www.fascinatingfactsforkids.com

Contents

Introduction

Abraham Lincoln came from humble beginnings, but his intelligence, ambition, courage, and sense of justice helped him become one the greatest ever presidents of the United States, although many would argue that he was the greatest.

He didn't attend school much as a boy, but his love of learning saw him become a successful lawyer as well as a politician.

On becoming president, Lincoln was to lead his country through a long and bloody war before becoming the first American president to be assassinated.

I hope the facts about Abraham Lincoln in this book will fascinate you and encourage you to find out even more about this remarkable man.

Max Rogers
May 2014

Early Life

1.   Abraham Lincoln was born on February 12, 1809, in a log cabin on a farm near Hodgenville, Kentucky. He was the second child of Thomas and Nancy Lincoln.

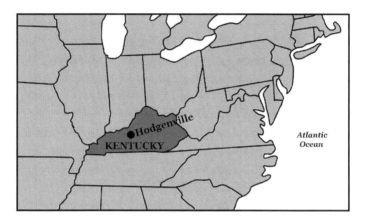

2.   Abraham was named after his grandfather, who had been shot dead during an Indian raid twenty-three years earlier in 1786.

3.   Thomas Lincoln was a well-respected, hard-working farmer, and when Abraham was old enough, he started to help out on the farm.

4.   Nancy, Abraham's mother, was a quiet woman who couldn't read, and she knew that it was important that her children got an education.

5.   Abraham and his sister, Sarah, used to regularly walk the two miles (3.2 km) to the nearest school where he developed his love of learning and reading.

6.   Abraham's father was a wealthy man, owning farms and cattle, but this was to change dramatically in 1816, when he lost all his land in a legal dispute.

7.   The Lincoln family was now facing poverty and moved to Indiana to make a fresh start. Although land was cheap there, it was covered in thick forest, so the Lincolns had to chop down trees to clear the land for a farm and to build a home to live in.

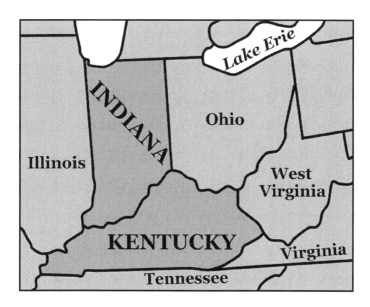

8.   It was hard work, and even when the land was ready to be farmed there was still constant work to be done. Abraham helped his father, and even though he was only eight years old he could use an ax. He even shot a turkey for the family dinner, although he hated doing this and vowed he would never kill anything again.

Abraham Loses His Mother

9.   In the summer of 1818, a terrible disease spread through the area. Abraham's mother was affected by the illness and died at the age of just thirty-four. Abraham was not even ten years old and had lost his mother.

10.   Abraham's sister, Sarah, who was just two years older than him, took over the cooking and cleaning while he and his father worked on the farm. She found it very hard and was often in tears.

11.   A year after his wife's death Abraham's father married again, to an old friend called Sarah Bush Johnston, and she and her three children came to live in the Lincoln family home.

12.   Abraham liked his new stepmother, who people called Sally. She was a kind woman and took over the running of the home from Sarah.

13.   Abraham was a good worker on the farm, but he went to school whenever his father could do without him. He learned to read and write, and always carried a book with him so that he could read whenever he had a spare moment.

14.   Abraham grew up into a strong, fit, and tall young man - he was over six feet tall by the time he was sixteen!

New Orleans & the Slave Market

15. When Abraham was seventeen he started to work for a ferryboat business on the nearby Ohio River. He also did some carpentry and was soon earning around six dollars a month.

16. A couple of years later, Abraham and another young man called Allen Gentry were hired to take a boat full of supplies down the Mississippi River to New Orleans, a city over 1,000 miles (1,600 km) away.

17. The Mississippi is the fourth-longest river in the world and the longest in America. It was a dangerous journey to make, but the two young men finally made it to New Orleans, surviving an attack by robbers on the way!

18. It was in New Orleans that Abraham first witnessed slaves being bought and sold, and he didn't like what he saw.

19. Slavery was commonplace in the southern United States in Lincoln's day. Thousands of Africans were transported across the Atlantic Ocean to work on the cotton plantations of their new American masters. Later in his life, Abraham was to dramatically change this situation.

African slaves on a plantation

New Salem & War

20. In 1832, at the age of twenty-two, Lincoln moved to the village of New Salem, Illinois, where he ran a general store. He liked New Salem and was to live there for six years, earning money doing a variety of jobs. He always made time for reading and learning though.

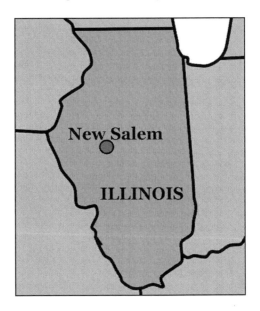

21. It was in New Salem that Lincoln became interested in the law. He used to go to the courthouse to see justice in action, and the court officials often asked him to help with some of the legal work. It was soon obvious that Lincoln had a talent for the law, and he decided to study to become a lawyer.

22. Lincoln obviously had brains, but he also had brawn. He was a fine wrestler and held his own with the toughest of opponents. He went on to become a champion wrestler, fighting over 300 times and losing just one match.

23. In 1832, there was a dispute over land between the United States and some Native American Indians and war was declared. Lincoln, along with many other young men, volunteered to fight and he was made captain of his company. Although the war was over very quickly and Lincoln didn't see any fighting, it did give him his first taste of leadership.

Lawyer & Politician

24. Lincoln was encouraged to go into politics at this time and although his first election campaign ended in defeat, he didn't give up. In his next attempt in August 1834, he won and was elected as a politician for the state of Illinois. Abraham Lincoln's political career had begun.

25. Lincoln passed his law exams in 1836, and the next year he moved the fifteen miles (24 km) from New Salem to the town of Springfield, where he began work as a lawyer. Combining politics and the law, he became well respected and was known as "Honest Abe."

26. Lincoln became a very successful lawyer and loved his work. The job also helped with his political career as it involved a lot of traveling, making him well-known to the voters of the area.

27. Slavery at the time was a big issue in the United States. The southern states relied on slavery for their economies but the "Abolitionists," who were mainly from the northern states, wanted it made illegal. When the United States was founded, it was declared that all men should be treated equally, but black slaves were obviously not included in this principle.

28. Lincoln was opposed to slavery and in 1837, when the government of the state of Illinois held a debate on the subject, he voted to make it illegal. It was a brave thing to do as only five other people out of eighty-three voted the same way. Lincoln wouldn't give in, though, and he was to return to the subject of slavery in later years.

Marriage & a Family

29. In 1839 Abraham met a twenty-one-year-old young woman called Mary Todd. They soon fell in love with each other and Abraham proposed the next year.

Mary Todd

30. The two people were different in many ways. Unlike Abraham, Mary came from a wealthy, slave-owning family and had been given a good education. They had much in common, though - they both had strong personalities and shared a love of politics and poetry.

31. A few weeks after proposing to Mary, Abraham called the engagement off. It may have been because Mary's family was not happy about her marrying someone from Abraham's background. Whatever the reason Abraham was very unhappy about it.

32. Mary wrote to Abraham saying that she still loved him and they started seeing each other again. There was no calling off of the engagement this time and the couple were married in August 1842.

33. The following year their first son, Robert, was born and a few months later they were able to buy their first house in Springfield. Abraham and Mary had three more sons, William, Edward and Tad, but Robert was the only one to survive into adulthood.

The Lincoln family home at Springfield

Congressman Lincoln

34. Lincoln served as a politician in Illinois until he was married, after which he decided to concentrate fully on his law practice.

35. He planned to enter national politics, though, and in 1846 he was elected to the House of Representatives, which meant that the family had to move to capital city of Washington, where the United States government is based.

36. The United States government, known as "Congress," consists of two houses - the House of Representatives and the Senate. A Member of the House of Representatives represents the people of a local district, and each state is represented by two Senators in the Senate.

37. Lincoln was a tireless and effective congressman and tried to make laws that would get rid of slavery in Washington. He had seen the slave markets in the city and his distaste for slavery was growing even stronger.

38. Lincoln served as a congressman in Washington for two years before moving back to Springfield to resume being a lawyer.

Defeat

39. By the 1850s, the northern and southern states of the United States had become very different from each other, and the main difference was the issue of slavery. Slavery was illegal in much of the North, but the South depended on slaves to work on the farms and plantations. The issue was threatening to split the United States of America in two.

40. Lincoln was against slavery, but he also wanted to keep the United States together. He entered politics again in 1854 to tackle these issues.

41. In 1855 Lincoln ran unsuccessfully for election to the Senate. This defeat led to him join a new political party, the Republican Party, which - like Lincoln - was opposed to slavery.

42. In 1858 the Republican Party chose Lincoln to run for Senator of Illinois. To get to the Senate he would have to beat the existing senator, Stephen Douglas, in an election.

Stephen Douglas

43. As part of the election campaign, the two men held a series of debates in cities across Illinois. The main topic of these debates was slavery, and Lincoln and Douglas were heard by thousands of people and reported in the newspapers.

44. When the election came, the voters chose Douglas as their senator, but the debates had made Lincoln well-known across America.

45. Lincoln thought that this defeat would end his political career, but he had impressed the other members of the Republican Party so much that they asked him to be their candidate for president.

President Lincoln

46. Lincoln would once more stand against Stephen Douglas and whoever won this election would become president of the United States of America.

47. Lincoln began his election campaign to try to persuade the people of America to vote for him. It was clear from the start that the northern states supported him but he was hated by the slave states of the South.

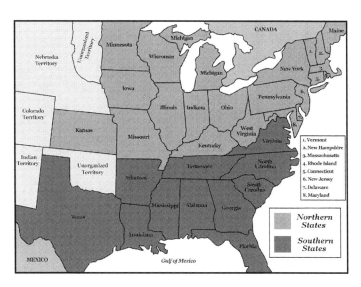

48. Lincoln won the election on November 6, 1860, and became president, but nearly all his votes came from the North with hardly any from the South. It looked like his dream of keeping the United States together was in ruins.

49. In the weeks following Lincoln's victory, seven southern states decided to separate from the North, and they joined together to form the Confederate States of America. The Confederates elected a president of their own, Jefferson Davies.

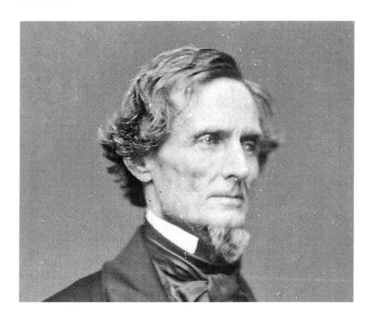

Jefferson Davis

50. Lincoln was desperate to avoid a war between the northern states, which were called the "Union," and the Confederates, but on April 12, 1861, a Confederate army attacked a Unionist fort at Charleston, South Carolina. The American Civil War had begun.

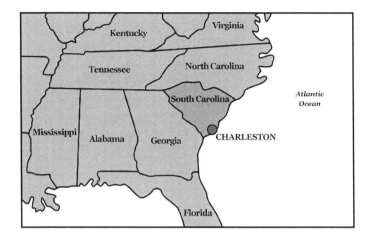

51. Wars are usually fought between different countries, but civil wars are perhaps even worse, as these involve people from the same country fighting against each other.

The Civil War

52. With the war now underway, thousands of volunteers rushed to join the armies of both the Union and the Confederacy. As president, Lincoln took complete charge of the war and, with the approval of Congress, gave himself powers that no previous president had possessed.

53. The "Battle of Bull Run," which took place on July 21, 1861, was the first major battle of the war. It resulted in defeat for the Union Army, and hundreds of men from both sides died. Lincoln did not sleep that night as details of the battle reached him.

The "Battle of Bull Run"

54. Following the Battle of Bull Run, there was little action between the opposing armies and some people thought that Lincoln might not be up to the job of war leader as he couldn't get his army to fight!

55. Lincoln was not impressed by some of the generals who led the Union Army, and he replaced them regularly. He began to read books about military strategy so that he could make the difficult decisions himself.

56. The real fighting began in 1862, but for three years Lincoln's generals failed to overcome the southern Army. All this changed when Lincoln appointed a new general, Ulysses S. Grant. Grant won battle after battle, and the South surrendered on April 9, 1865. The American Civil War was finally over.

Ulysses S. Grant

57. After four years of bloodshed and with over 600,000 deaths on both sides, America would be united again. Lincoln had also achieved his goal of abolishing slavery when, on January 31, 1865, Congress passed a law making slavery illegal across the whole of the United States of America.

The Gettysburg Address

58. Perhaps the most famous battle of the American Civil war was the "Battle of Gettysburg," which lasted for three days in July 1863. 51,000 men were killed or injured at Gettysburg in an important victory for the Union.

The "Battle of Gettysburg"

59. After the battle, Lincoln traveled to Gettysburg to honor the men who had died and he gave a speech to a crowd of 20,000 people. The speech, known as the "Gettysburg Address," lasted less than three minutes during which Lincoln gave his reasons why the war was so important for the freedom and equality of everyone in America. The speech *(overleaf)* has become one of the most important in the history of the United States.

"Four score and seven years ago our fathers brought forth on this continent a new nation, conceived in liberty, and dedicated to the proposition that all men are created equal.

Now we are engaged in a great civil war, testing whether that nation, or any nation so conceived and so dedicated, can long endure. We are met on a great battlefield of that war. We have come to dedicate a portion of that field, as a final resting place for those who here gave their lives that that nation might live. It is altogether fitting and proper that we should do this.

But, in a larger sense, we can not dedicate, we can not consecrate, we can not hallow this ground. The brave men, living and dead, who struggled here, have consecrated it, far above our poor power to add or detract. The world will little note, nor long remember what we say here, but it can never forget what they did here. It is for us the living, rather, to be dedicated here to the unfinished work which they who fought here have thus far so nobly advanced. It is rather for us to be here dedicated to the great task remaining before us - that from these honored dead we take increased devotion to that cause for which they gave the last full measure of devotion - that we here highly resolve that these dead shall not have died in vain - that this nation, under God, shall have a new birth of freedom - and that government of the people, by the people, for the people, shall not perish from the earth."

Lincoln's Death

60. Five days after the South's surrender, Lincoln and his wife, Mary, were due to visit the Ford's Theater in Washington to see a play. They arrived late and although the play had already started, the audience stood up to cheer the president, who then sat down to enjoy the show.

61. Around ninety minutes later, John Wilkes Booth, a confederate who hated Lincoln, entered the president's box and crept up behind him. He pulled out a gun, aimed it at the president's head and pulled the trigger.

62. As Lincoln slumped forward, Booth jumped out of the box onto the stage below and although he broke a leg as he did so, he still managed to escape. He was on the run for twelve days before being caught and killed in a struggle.

Lincoln's assassination

63. The president was taken from the theater to a house across the street where doctors did what they could to save him. But there was nothing they could do and Lincoln died at 7.22 the next morning.

64. Lincoln was the first United States president to have been assassinated and America was in shock. Thousands of people came to Washington from all over the country to pay their respects.

65. Lincoln's body was taken home to Illinois by train. Hundreds of thousands of people lined the track and attended memorial services on the journey. He was buried in Springfield on May 3, 1865.

Abraham Lincoln's tomb in Springfield

Conclusion

Lincoln led his country through the most difficult period in its history. The war saw a huge loss of life as Americans fought their fellow Americans. And when the war was over there was the enormous task of rebuilding the country to tackle.

Although Lincoln had given black men and women their freedom with the abolition of slavery, there was a long way to go before they were treated as equals. Despite these problems, Lincoln's great achievement of abolishing slavery in America began the long process of equal rights for everyone.

Lincoln was a great president and his greatness was recognized on his death bed. Edwin Stanton, the Secretary of War said simply, "There lies the most perfect ruler of men the world has ever seen."

Illustration Attributions

Title page
Alexander Gardner [Public domain]

African slaves on a plantation
Civil War Treasures from the New-York
Historical Society, [Digital ID, e.g., nhnycw/ad
ad04004] [Public domain]

House of Representatives seal (Fact 35)
Ipankonin [Public domain]

Jefferson Davies | Ulysses S. Grant
www.goodfreephotos.com

The "Battle of Bull Run"
Kurz & Allison [Public domain]
{{PD-US}}

The "Battle of Gettysburg"
Adam Cuerden
{{PD-US}}

Lincoln's assassination
Currier and Ives [Public domain]